CONTENTS

Table of Content	6
ThE CD Baby's thank you email	7
Piz-Zappos with extra toppings	11
A different spin to, "Houston, we have a problem"	14
The everyday superheros of planet earth	17
Customer support with role plays are twice as fun	22
Charity begins at Wegmans	26
Meet Little Mia's Own Flynn Rider	29
Who rules the world?	33
The best kind of wedding crashers	36

7 Great Customer Stories Of All Time To Melt Your Heart

Written by Manish Nepal

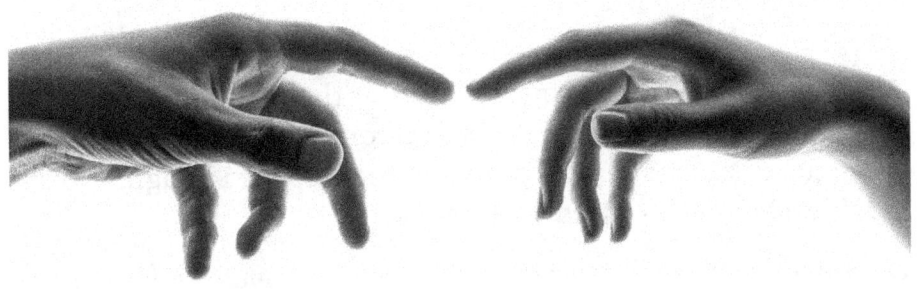

What pops in your head when you close your eyes and think of customer service?

Let me guess.

It would be either a smiling twenty-something poster girl in a call centre talking at her headset mic.

Or the 1-800 phonewords and never-ending wait time.

Or maybe Santa Claus?

Hospital nurses?

Your mom?

For me, it's the lifeless Samsung headset that I bought online last year, which is gathering dust in one corner of my bookshelf because the customer service people of the website I bought it from didn't exchange or refund it for me. ☹

Of course, my memory is biased because I have a tendency to remember only the experiences that were either personally hurting or overwhelmingly great.

Unfortunately, the latter have remained a rarity in my life when it comes to experiencing outstanding customer service.

But when I do come across a good customer service experience, it pattern- interrupts my attention and takes me by a pleasant surprise.

My brain has a mushy corner for stories about happy endings, sob stories, and amazing act of kindness.

I personally encountered two incidents recently that inspired me to write on this topic:

1. The utmost hospitality I got from the employees at a bike repair shop when I went to pick up my bike

2. The 60% refund I received on a hunting cap that I had purchased from a sporting goods store because they had priced it incorrectly

It's important to clarify that the response from both these brands were voluntary; I didn't provoke them to elicit such behaviors. I merely presented my issue in a matter-of-fact way but received amazing service in return when I least expected it.

Those "wow" experiences opened the floodgates of all the incredible customer service stories that I have heard or read about.

As you are about to find our, these are not my first-hand experiences. But just reading about these stories time and again have streaked beautifully in my mind. Now, they are all screaming to come out to the world.

They deserve repeated re-broadcasts because of how great they are.

It's my hope that they inspire other businesses to develop a culture of legendary customer service.

So here it is...a list of my all-time favorite customer stories—ranked in the order of goosebumps they give you.

TABLE OF CONTENT

1. CDBaby's thank you email 5

2. Piz-Zappos with extra toppings 8

3. "Houston, we have a problem" 10

4. The everyday superheros of planet earth 13

5. Thor goes to Odin for help 18

6. Charity begins at Wegmans 22

7. Meet Mia's own Flynn Rider 25

8. Who rules the world? 29

9. The best kind of wedding crashers 32

THE CD BABY'S THANK YOU EMAIL

Derek Sivers started CDBaby.com after spending 10 years of his life working as a circus clown.

No kidding.

So it's only natural for him to carry over some extent of humor when he began selling CDs online. And what happened when he combined humor with business?

Here's the result:

> Thank you for your order with CD Baby!
>
> Your CD has been gently taken from our CD Baby shelves with sterilized contamination-free gloves and placed onto a satin pillow.
>
> A team of 50 employees inspected your CD and polished it to make sure it was in the best possible condition before mailing.
>
> Our packing specialist from Japan lit a candle and a hush fell over the crowd as he put your CD into the finest gold-lined box that money can buy.
>
> We all had a wonderful celebration afterwards and the whole party marched down the street to the post office where the entire town of Portland waved "Bon Voyage!" to your package, on its way to you, in our private CD Baby jet on this day, Friday, June 6th.
>
> I hope you had a wonderful time shopping at CD Baby. We sure did. Your picture is on our wall as "Customer of the Year." We're all exhausted but can't wait for you to come back to CDBABY.COM!!
>
> Thank you once again
>
> Derek Sivers, president, CD Baby
> the little store with the best new independent music

Tickles you pink, doesn't it?

But here's my favorite part of this story: Derek ran CD Baby from his apartment for several years.

For the most part of his initial success, he didn't have other people handling his inventory, marketing, or customer service.

Combine that with the fact that CDBaby.com was born during the late 90s, in the thick of the dot com boom, and you can conclude that customer service wasn't exactly a priority for him.

Businesses in the 90s didn't put so much value on customer service as much as sales and marketing.

Sivers didn't need to write an email that would cause people to feel special about shopping with CDBaby.

He could have written a boring acknowledgement and be done with it.

He would have still enjoyed the profits because CDBaby at the time was the lone wolf in the online music selling business for a long time.

And yet, Sivers felt compelled to create an email that swept his customers' feet and created a ripple we still feel today—years after Sivers has moved away from CDBaby to answer other callings of life.

What Derek did as a one-man business has left an indelible mark in the world of customer service and raised the bar for others to follow suit.

Fun fact: Derek sold CD Baby to another company for $22 million in 2008 and donated the majority of it to The Independent Musician's Charitable Trust.

*"Five years after I started CD Baby, when it was a big success, the media said I had revolutionized the music business.

But 'revolution' is a term that people use only when you're successful.

Before that, you're just a quirky person who does things differently."*

— Derek Sivers

PIZ-ZAPPOS WITH EXTRA TOPPINGS

The stories of Zappos' customer support are so legendary, so good to be true, that most of them sound like straight-up urban myths.

Where do we begin talking about them?

The time when the company saved a groomsman from being barefoot at his own wedding?

When the support reps send a basket of white lilies with a thoughtful card to a grieving customer who had lost her mother?

Or when Zappos' CEO prank-called his customer service late at night to get help with midnight pizza delivery?

Let's settle with the third one because it has a lot of pizzazz to it.

Tony Hsieh, Zappos' co-founder and erstwhile CEO was meeting executives from Skechers at a bar after a conference one night.

We all know what happens when businesspeople gather to discuss on important agendas, right?

Unsurprisingly, the business talks took longer than they had planned for, by which time the bar stopped serving food.

It must have been close to midnight when they reached their hotel. But the hotel's room service had shut their kitchen for the night as well.

That's when Tony came up with a prank idea and prodded his hungry clients to call Zappos' customer care to get help with ordering pizza.

The Skechers execs took the dare and called the Zappos' customer service, put the call on speaker, and explained their predicament.

The customer service rep who took the call patiently heard the caller's story, asked him about his whereabouts, and put him on hold briefly.

Barely a minute later, the rep gave the caller phone numbers of pizza parlors who took late night delivery orders near his hotel.

I can imagine the other men in the hotel room exchanging admiring glances with each other while they high-fived Tony.

What's so beautiful about this story is that instead of refusing to entertain an irrelevant service call, the service rep did what was in his/her capacity to help a starving customer order his pizza.

And what an immense sense of pride—instilling that kind of serving culture—Tony must have felt in that moment!

If only all frontend reps had thiskind of problem-solving mindset, we would live in a utopia where all drunk-dialled pizza orders would always be delivered.

A DIFFERENT SPIN TO, "HOUSTON, WE HAVE A PROBLEM"

United Airlines gets more flak than flattery for the controversies it creates.

Drawing unwanted attention is almost becoming an industry standard for airline businesses, and United Airlines leads from the front.

Just a couple of years ago, it made big headlines for violently dragging a middle- aged passenger out of the flight because he wouldn't volunteer to give up his seat for overbooked flight.

But we have to give props where it's due—the airlines' past customer service records are not so bad.

Just hear it out from Kerry Drake who was flying from San Francisco, CA to catch a connecting flight in Houston, TX to see his mother who was counting her last moments in Lubbock, TX.

Drake had an impossible 40-minute layover time in Houston to catch the last flight for that day to Lubbock.

Mid-flight, the pilot of the UA flight 667 en route Houston announced over the P.A. that their landing in Houston was delayed.

Drake thought he was not going to make it on time to talk to his mother for one last time and he broke down.

The sight of a grown man crying drew the flight crew's attention who not only comforted him for the rest of the flight but also radioed the pilot of the United Flight to Lubbock.

Upon landing, Drake lost no time in dashing towards the flight departure gate.

A few meters away from the gate, a UA gate exec stood there smiling, and said, "Mr. Drake? We have been expecting you."

She let him through the gate without even checking his boarding pass.

Unbeknownst to Drake, the UA crew had collaborated to delay the flight by 15 minutes and held the door open.

This was a rare and risky move by the UA flight crew because airline companies are known to be aggressive about their schedule.

They even ensured Drake's luggage arrived in the Lubbock airport along with him.

They went out of their way to help a distraught passenger meet his dying mother before it was too late.

Drake made it on time to spent the last few precious moments with his mother who breathed her last the following morning.

THE EVERYDAY SUPERHEROS OF PLANET EARTH

What's the definition of superheroes?

> *Benevolent people who possess extraordinary strength, courage, and wisdom to help people and make the world a better place for everyone.*

That's right. The qualification for being a superhero is not a superhuman physical strength or radioactive spider bite, but the selflessness to help others around them.

I believe some of the best superheroes we have don't live in the Marvel comic books or in the silver screen.

You don't notice them because they don't don capes or sport underpants above their spandex costumes. They are not filthy rich like Bruce Wayne or Tony Stark. Most of them don't even realize they are doing superhero deeds.

These superheroes go undetected because they are busy serving tables at restaurants or ringing groceries for customers in the supermarket cash counters.

Yes, some of the kickass superheros we have in this world are minimal wage workers who survive at the lowest rung of the employment food chain.

And yet, they possess extraordinary courage to serve humanity and give amazing customer service when their duty calls.

We can't do justice to all of the everyday heroes out there, but here is a tribute to a few of them who have managed to steal the limelight in the prime time.

We will start with Evoni Williams, the WaPe House waitress at La Marque, TX who slowed down her usual speed of attending multiple tables to assist an elderly customer.

The customer, an octogenarian patient recovering from a recent medical surgery, had an oxygen tank to assist his breathing and lacked the necessary motor skills to cut the ham he had ordered.

When he asked 18-year-old Williams for help, she quickly leaned over the counter, without a second thought, and helped him with his request.

A customer who witnessed this act of kindness took a photo of Williams helping her customer and posted it on her Facebook page.

By evening, the photo went viral and ended up giving a little something to everyone involved—a lifetime of memories for the elderly customer (and other customers who were moved by the incident), $16,000 college scholarship to Williams, and a day dedicated on her name by the city Mayor.

And of course, a great PR to Waffle House.

Here's a photo that went viral on Facebook.

That happened in April of 2018.

If you travel down 40 miles southwest from La Marque and 10 months into the future, you will come to H-E-B supermarket in Lake Jackson, TX where Jake Pate works.

Like other superheroes, Jake doesn't strike as an extraordinary human to people waiting in the checkout lane. But what he did recently broke the internet momentarily.

A few days before Christmas, Jake rang up a lady who, he discovered, was short of money for all the items she had placed in the cash counter. Jake decided to help.

Not wanting to hold up the line, Jake pulled out his wallet, swiped his card, and casually said "Merry Christmas" to the lady.

Here's Jake the Superhero:

But there's another heartwarming backstory to what Jake did. According to Jake, he was simply passing on the good deed because he saw the same woman that he helped pay for someone else's grocery!

That's not all. There's another follow-up story to that.

A good Samaritan, Shannon Whitley, awarded Jake a $5,000 scholarship for his act of "showing up" for a good cause. Kindness is just like a daisy chain that keeps on dovetailing.

CUSTOMER SUPPORT WITH ROLE PLAYS ARE TWICE AS FUN

The high mandate on digital transformation is pushing all businesses to move from bricks to clicks.

The majority of customer service experiences these days happen at online storefronts, not inside airlines aisles or supermarket checkout lanes.

While there are barriers to delivering great customer service over the internet, there is no dearth of stellar customer service stories in the vast swaths of cyber-land.

And we can't talk about amazing customer support in the context of online business without mentioning live chat, now can we?

And if that live chat customer support happens to involve Thor who is trying to help his father Odin, it makes up it an epic moment in the history of customer support. Take a look:

Chat

You are now connected to Amazon from Amazon.com

Me: Tracking shows delivered by shipment not recieved

Amazon: Warmest greetings ▮▮▮, my name is Thor.

Me: Greeting, Thor. Can I be Odin?

Amazon: Odin, Father, How art thy doing on this here fine day?

Me: Thor, my son. Agony raises upon my life

Amazon: This is outrageous! Who dares defy The All Father Odin! What has occured to cause this agony?

Me: I am afraid the book I ordered to defeat our enemies has been misplaced. How can we keep Valhalla intact without our sacred book.

Amazon: This is blasphemy! Wherever this book has been taken to, I shall make it my duty to get it back to you! I fear it is Loki but I dare not blame him for such things. I shall have your fortune retuned to you and thereafter we can begin to create a new quest in order to get the book back to you.

Me: Very well my son.

Amazon: Allow me some time to round up my allies and complete this please Father.

Me: Do it for me Thor, but most importantly do it for the mortals whose destiny (and grades) rely on this book.

Amazon: Alas, the treasure has been returned to you. You now need to reinstate the book into your archive so that you may yet receive it soon.
I shall have the Valkyrie deliver it to you as fast as their wings can move.

Me: Ok so roleplay aside I have my money back and I reorder the book?

Amazon: haha yes I have refunded you and you need to reorder the book.

Me: Great!

Amazon: Have you placed that order?

Me: let me do that.
done

Amazon: Okey let me edit it for you
▮▮▮▮▮▮▮▮▮▮
That good?

Me: Wow hooking me up with one day delivery? Sweet!

Amazon: haha yeah man gotta get your book asap!

Me: Ive heard Amazon had great customer service and this just proves it! thanks man

Amazon: No problem ▮▮▮. Is there any other issue or question that i can help you with?

Me: Nah that was it. Really appreciate it

Amazon: Anytime bro. Have a great day. Goodbye Odin

Me: Bye my son

It's because of these legendary customer service instances that makes me want to start a petition to rename Amazon's customer service as Amazing Customer Service!

Jokes aside, Amazon walks the talk when it comes to its customer-first approach. When Amazon's CEO Jeff Bezos says, "we are not competitor obsessed, we are customer obsessed"—we don't doubt it for a second.

Amazon will replace your order if the delivery package gets lost or is misplaced in transit. If you have a complaint or an issue, you can use one of the many available options to contact the support department.

And live chat happens to be the personal favorite of customers as well as service reps because it's faster and offers fun on both sides.

Here's another example of how a support rep from Netflix pretends to be Captain Mike (of Star Trek) to help out a customer, who volunteers as Lt. Norm to report a problem.

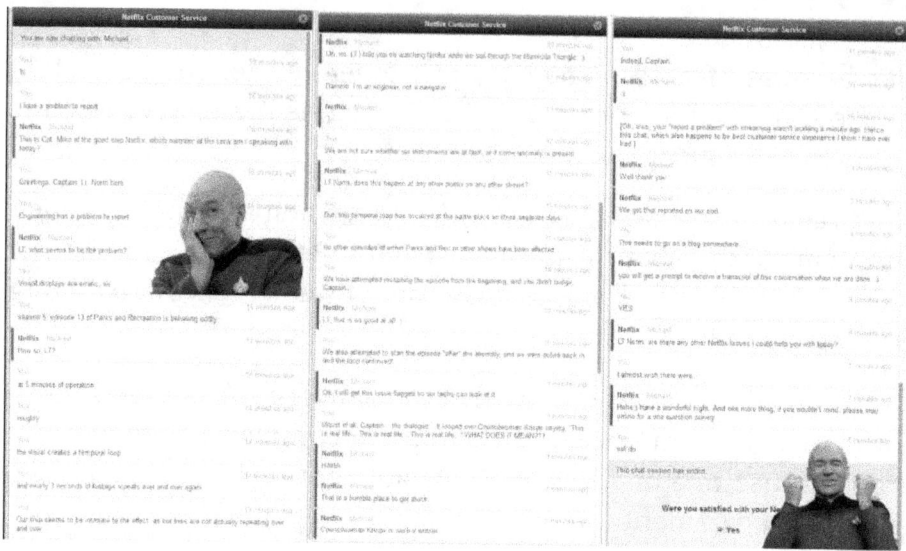

A kind interaction with a stranger is one of the best highs we can experience.

Live chat is just great, but we can see examples of great service like the ones mentioned above in social media all the time.

Customer support on Facebook or Twitter, for example, is quick and personalized. Airlines cos. such as Alaska Air, Virgin America, and JetBlue Airways respond to customer queries on Twitter in a matter of 4–5 minutes.

CHARITY BEGINS AT WEGMANS

The customer service stories of Wegmans', the Buffalo-based food retailer is so legendary that...it has inspired a broadway musical, it is voted among the best companies for customer service in a row, and actor Alec Baldwin's mother once refused to relocate from Syracuse, NY to Los Angeles, CA because she didn't want to move away from Wegmans'.

Oh yes, they all sound like myths. A utopian food chain from a parallel universe.

Customers can't stop raving about how excellent their customer service is and how everybody in Wegmans is so warm and knowledgeable.

But the kind of exemplary customer service that I want to highlight in the context of Wegmans is slightly different.

For me, the extraordinary customer service that Wegmans provides trumps everyone else's because they are an employee-first business.

Their first customers are their employees.

The business genuinely cares for its staff, their families, and their development which eventually shines through their customer service.

Wegmans offers a great employee experience which in turn improves their customer service.

The company wins accolades for being not just a company for excellent customer service but also for being their best employer in the U.S. How many companies in the world are able to bag both of those titles in the same year?

Wegmans is the rarified of rarified grocery chains to offer healthcare coverage for its 48,000 strong employees.

The company spends about $4.5 million in tuition and scholarships every year to support its staff that are enrolled in college.

> "The [employee] benefits include discounted movie tickets, theme park tickets, and select gym memberships," a Wegmans cashier once wrote in an anonymous Reddit post.

When Wegmans opened up a new store in Philadelphia, it was swarmed with more than 10,000 job applications for the 500 openings it had advertised for.

Considering the cult-like following around Wegmans and people's strong fandom to work for the company, no wonder the a Fortune magazine report once found that one in every five employees across Wegmans stores are related.

MEET LITTLE MIA'S OWN FLYNN RIDER

One of the things on the very top of our family's bucket list is to take our daughter to visit Disneyland—the happiest place on earth—for her to experience some magical pixie dust magic.

And it's not just because it's paradise on earth filled with all the amazing fictional characters you can hug and take photographs with.

Disneyland is known for creating magic in the lives of the 18 million visitors who throng there every year. If you want to picture how does that look on an everyday basis—it's 50,000 people daily.

Give or take another 2000–3000 people who ebb and tide based on the peak and low season respectively.

The Disneyland ~~employees~~ sorry..."cast members," are super-friendly. They will jump to your help dressed as Elsa, Jasmine, or Aladdin across all sections of the park.

Just listen to this heartwarming story of a dad who took his 18-month-old daughter to Disneyland in 2015 for a Tangled-themed wedding.

"In 2015, we attended the wedding of dear friends at Disney World. They had this absolutely stunning Tangled-themed wedding. Flynn and Rapunzel even stopped by to meet the guests and wish the couple well.

Our daughter was only 18 months at the time, but was super into Flynn. He kept coming back to her between photos, and folks had to keep reminding him to get into photos with the other guests. Our little one absolutely loved him and decided he was 'her Flynn.'

We went back to Disney a little over a year later and booked breakfast to eat with Ariel, Prince Eric, Rapunzel, and Flynn at The Boardwalk resort.

We mentioned to the hostess how excited our daughter was to see Flynn again after their first meeting was so special. Well, clearly some magic happened since not much later, Flynn made a special trip out to see our daughter.

He walked up to her saying, "Where's my Mia?"

She lit up!

She truly believes, to this day, that he remembered her from the wedding. She got a beautiful light-up Pascal for free, and she and Flynn colored a very special picture together for Rapunzel and presented it to her in front of the other guests."

— mandyb48a9ecf6b (from BuzzFeed)

Mia, the kiddo was obsessed with the charming Flynn Rider, and although the toddler couldn't speak much, her love for Flynn was very obvious in her eyes.

The Cast Member paid back the adoration and kept visiting Mia between taking photos with other guests in the party.

Enamored with Flynn's attention to her, Mia, in her cute special toddler-entitled way, staked the claim that he was "her Flynn."

But that's not the happy ending. When the family visited the theme park a year later, Mia's memory of Flynn was still very alive in her heart. The family adults tipped the Cast Members about how crazy their little daughter was about Flynn and—lo and behold—a few moments later, a new Flynn Rider walked up to the little one and said:

"Where's my Mia?"

Disneyland had showered Mia with its magical fairy dust all over again.

In young Mia's mind, it was "her Flynn" who she had met the year before. Her Flynn came because he remembered her from last year's wedding. Later, Flynn helped her make a painting and gifted her a nice little Pascal as a farewell gift.

It's stories like this from Disneyland and the Disney World that make me think—what kind of world would it had been if the Imagineer-in-chief Walt Disney was able to create the Disney-themed city that he had envisioned?

If his vision of Disney parks are able to deliver such ecstatic moments of magic, imagine what a magical place that city would have been?

While I may or may not end up taking my daughter there, I hope to keep hearing stories like this to experience the Disney magic from my armchair.

WHO RULES THE WORLD?

Girls.

That's not just a catchy line from Beyoncé's song, but a fact. Girls—especially little girls like Mia—rule the world, hands down.

Want more proof? Say hello to Lily Robinson.

Lily was a feisty three-year-old who changed tigers into giraffes.

Well, not in the jungle, you know. But her ingenious idea got the UK's biggest supermarket store to change the name of their tiger brand breads to giraffe breads.

Here's how.

Lily noticed that the spots on the tiger bread didn't resemble the tiger stripes she had seen on TV of her school books.

Instead, the pattern was strikingly similar to the spots giraffes had on their body. So she wrote a letter to Sainsbury's customer service, stating:
"Why is tiger bread called tiger bread? It should be called giraffe bread."

I won't be able to do justice to the original message. Here's how it looks:

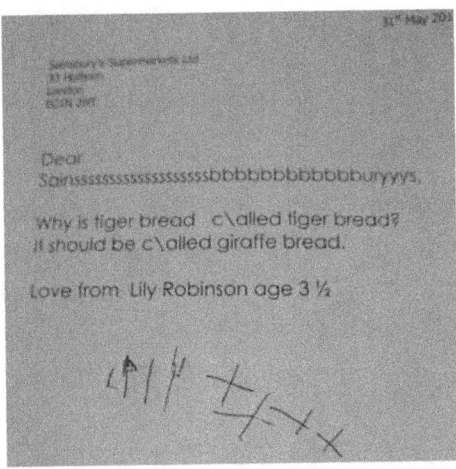

The customer service team lost no time in responding to Lily's inquiry. Here's the reply she received:

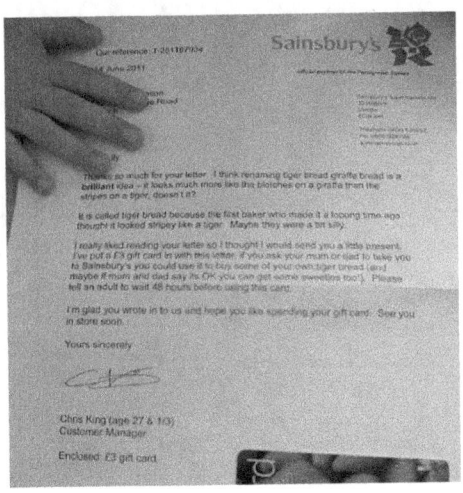

Lily got her reply and was rewarded for her idea—a gift card enclosed with the reply letter—but it didn't amount to anything much.

However, Lily's mother decided to have fun with the whole thing and she wrote a blog documenting the interaction her three-year-old had with the Sainsbury's support team.

The post blew up on Facebook—with over 150,000 likes and 48,000 shares—and soon Sainsbury's started to reel under the pressure of rechristening their bread.

The supermarket responded, "In response to overwhelming customer feedback that our tiger bread has more resemblance to a giraffe, from today we will be changing our tiger bread to giraffe bread and seeing how that goes."

Sainsbury's

We're renaming #tigerbread to #giraffebread thanks to Lily Robinson. RT if you'll be looking for it instore bit.ly/zsDAlz

So one fine day, the tiger bread was duly renamed as giraffe bread and Lily's name was etched in the book of Sainsburys history book in golden letters.

THE BEST KIND OF WEDDING CRASHERS

How many of us can say that we would be happy if somebody crashed our wedding?

Not an awful lot, if any. But I bet for a few couples from Los Angeles, CA are and will be forever nostalgic of that time when some people created a hullabaloo and crashed their wedding in the awesomest manner possible.

Yes, for my final number—I present to you the most charming wedding crashers...Maroon 5 the band!

In their music video for *Sugar*, the Adam Levine-led band is seen hopping on their convertible, going from one wedding venue to another across L.A. neighborhoods, making their way into the wedding halls from kitchen backdoors, and performing their song to the shocked crowd and the super-stoked brides and grooms.

Here's a still from the music video:

The video grabs my attention as the best kind of customer service because the band chose to surprise their fan on the most important days of their lives and make it more special.

It was a gift those fans will cherish for years and years and talk about it to their children and grandchildren.

And what a smart way for the band to market their new song/album release!

Now rumor has it that parts of these weddings were staged for the purpose of making this video, and it could be very well true.

(I wish I had the connections in Hollywood to verify its authenticity.)

But it looks like the grooms knew about the plan or plotted for it, while the brides are seen gasping and exclaiming "WTF" and "OMG".

Judging by that, my heart says the plan might have been premeditated on both sides, but there is a good chance it is real.

Staged or not, Maroon 5 definitely mic-dropped this act.

But Maroon 5 are not the only musical bands to pull of these great moments of "wows" for their fans.

The immediate other name that comes to mind is Foo Fighters, who step out of their stardom during live shows from time to time and give their fans a chance to perform with them.

This happened last year. And what's great about the whole gig is that the fan—Kiss Guy—absolutely nailed the performance while Dave Grohl and his boys had to collect their jaws from the floor later on.

Now that could have been a staged performance, if you ask me.

~The End~

Thank You For Buying This Ebook!

I hope you enjoyed reading the stories as much as I loved writing them.

I would appreciate it if you can rate and review this book.

If you have any suggestions, feedback, or queries—you can write to me at manishnepal.com@gmail.com.

You can also find me on Twitter or LinkedIn.

~ Manish Nepal

www.ingramcontent.com/pod-product-compliance
Lightning Source LLC
Chambersburg PA
CBHW070843220526
45466CB00002B/866